GERMANY

EXPLORE THE COUNTRIES

Sarah Tieck

Big Buddy BOOKS

Explore the Countries

VISIT US AT
www.abdopublishing.com

Published by ABDO Publishing Company, PO Box 398166, Minneapolis, MN 55439.

Printed in the United States of America, North Mankato, Minnesota.
042013
112013
♻ PRINTED ON RECYCLED PAPER

Coordinating Series Editor: Rochelle Baltzer
Contributing Editors: Megan M. Gunderson, Marcia Zappa
Graphic Design: Adam Craven
Cover Photograph: *Shutterstock*: Zbynek Jirousek.
Interior Photographs/Illustrations: *AP Photo*: AP Photo (pp. 15, 17), Lionel Cironneau (p. 15), DB Stiftung Weimarer Klassik/picture-alliance/dpa/AP Images (p. 31), Hannibal Hanschke/picture-alliance/dpa/AP Images (p. 19), North Wind Picture Archives via AP Images (pp. 13, 33), Ferdinand Ostrop (p. 23); *Getty Images*: Feargus Cooney (p. 21), EyesWideOpen (p. 35); *Glow Images*: Dani Carlo (p. 34), Hans Lippert (p. 29), imagebroker.com imagebroker/Hans Lippert (p. 25); *iStockphoto*: ©iStockphoto.com/nullplus (p. 29), ©iStockphoto.com/schenkArt (p. 27), ©iStockphoto.com/wakila (p. 27); *Shutterstock*: Karl Allgaeuer (p. 35), Globe Turner (pp. 19, 38), Harald Lueder (p. 35), Mirenska Olga (p. 34), Maryna Pleshkun (p. 38), PRILL (pp. 23, 37), Prometheus72 (p. 11), Tiberiu Stan (p. 16), Boris Stroujko (p. 5), tomtsya (p. 11), VICTOR TORRES (p. 9).

Country population and area figures taken from the CIA World Factbook.

Library of Congress Control Number: 2013932146

Cataloging-in-Publication Data

Tieck, Sarah.
  Germany / Sarah Tieck.
    p. cm. -- (Explore the countries)
  ISBN 978-1-61783-811-8 (lib. bdg.)
  1. Germany--Juvenile literature.   I. Title.
  943--dc23
                                                    2013932146

GERMANY

Contents

Around the World

Our world has many countries. Each country has beautiful land. It has its own rich history. And, the people have their own languages and ways of life.

Germany is a country in Europe. What do you know about Germany? Let's learn more about this place and its story!

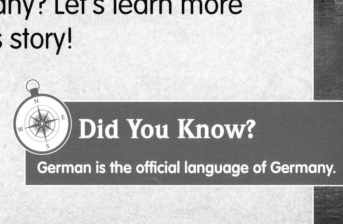

Did You Know?

German is the official language of Germany.

The Danube River starts in southern Germany. From there, it flows through eight other countries in Europe.

5

PASSPORT TO GERMANY

Germany is a country in central Europe. Nine countries border it. It is also bordered by the Baltic Sea and the North Sea.

Germany's total area is 137,847 square miles (357,022 sq km). More than 81 million people live there.

WHERE IN THE WORLD?

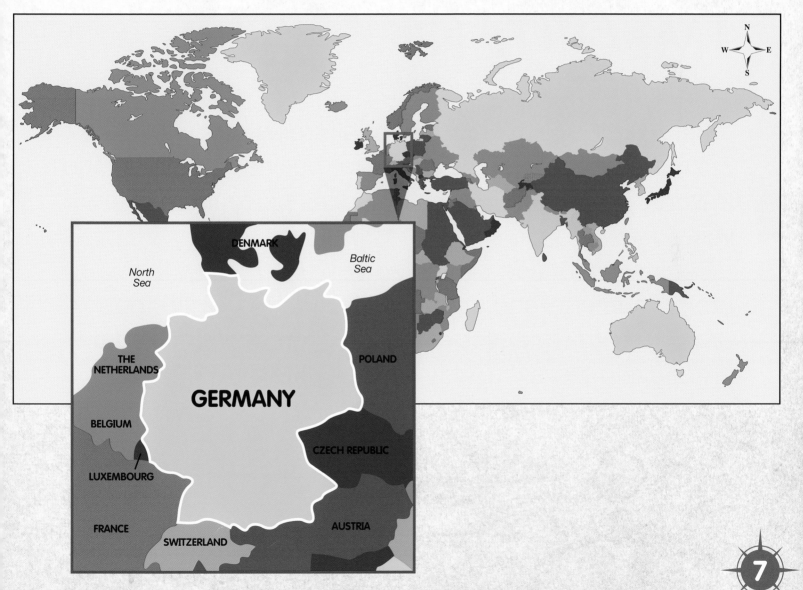

IMPORTANT CITIES

Berlin is Germany's **capital** and largest city, with about 3.4 million people. It is a center for business, politics, and the arts. The Berlin Film Festival takes place there every year.

Berlin was founded in the early 1200s. Today, there are monuments and museums to honor the city's past. Brandenburg Gate was completed in 1791. It marked an entrance to the city. Today it stands for German **unity** and is popular with visitors.

Did You Know?

In 1871, Berlin became the capital of the German Empire.

• Hamburg

Berlin ★

GERMANY

N
W E
S

Munich •

Berlin became Germany's capital in 1990 after East and West Germany were united.

Hamburg is Germany's second-largest city. It has about 1.7 million people. This port city is on the Elbe River, near the North Sea. The Alster River also flows through the city and forms two lakes. Hamburg is a center for German business, including newspapers.

Munich is Germany's third-largest city, with about 1.2 million people. This historic city is on the Isar River. Food products and electronics are made there.

> **SAY IT**
>
> **Munich**
> *MYOO-nick*

Hamburg's port is one of the largest in Europe.

The New Town Hall is a famous government building in Munich.

GERMANY IN HISTORY

Ancient Germany was ruled by tribes. Around the year 500, many of these groups **united** under the Franks. Charlemagne was a powerful Frankish ruler. In 800, he was crowned **emperor** of much of western Europe. He ruled until his death in 814.

Soon after, the eastern part of his **empire** became Germany. The country had several states with their own rulers.

In the late 1800s, many of Germany's states were united into the German Empire. This was called the Second Reich. Germany was a major power in Europe at this time.

Charlemagne's empire became known as the Holy Roman Empire.

13

After losing **World War** I, Germany lost power and colonies. In 1933, Adolf Hitler and the **Nazi** Party took control of Germany. Hitler wanted to create a new German **empire** called the Third Reich. This led to **World War** II.

In 1945, Germany lost the war. It was split into East and West Germany. Berlin was also split. East Germany and East Berlin were **Communist**. In 1961, the East German government built the Berlin Wall. This was to stop people from leaving to live in West Germany. The country **united** again in 1990.

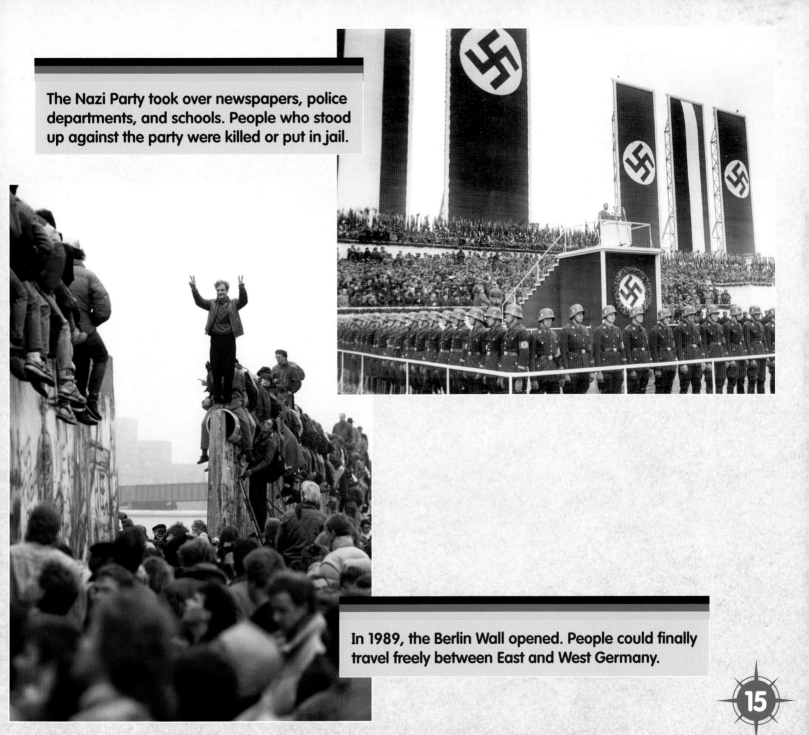

The Nazi Party took over newspapers, police departments, and schools. People who stood up against the party were killed or put in jail.

In 1989, the Berlin Wall opened. People could finally travel freely between East and West Germany.

Timeline

1685

Johann Sebastian Bach was born in Eisenach. He wrote hundreds of songs, including "Jesu, Joy of Man's Desiring." Some people consider him a musical genius.

1517

German monk Martin Luther began a movement called the Reformation. His ideas led to the formation of the Lutheran Church.

1868

In Bavaria, King Ludwig II began building Neuschwanstein Castle. Construction stopped in 1886, when the king died. Some people say it looks like a fairy-tale castle.

1939

Germany took over Poland. Two days later, Great Britain and France declared war. This began **World War II**. By the end of the war, **Nazis** had killed millions of people. This included about 6 million Jews as part of the **Holocaust**.

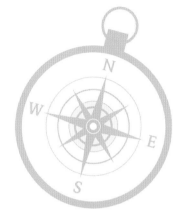

2010

Oktoberfest honored 200 years. The first one was held in Munich after a royal wedding in 1810. This festival usually happens from late September until the first Sunday in October.

1989

People began to tear down the Berlin Wall, which had stood since 1961.

An Important Symbol

Germany's flag was first used in the mid-1800s. It became the country's flag after **World War I** and again following **World War II**. The colors stand for German **unity**.

Germany's government is a **federal republic**. There are 16 states. Germany's parliament makes laws. The president is the head of state. The chancellor is the head of government.

Black, red, and gold are the national colors of Germany.

In 2005, Chancellor Angela Merkel took office. She became Germany's first female chancellor.

ACROSS THE LAND

Germany has mountains, coasts, river valleys, and flat areas. The Black Forest is in the southwest. Thick fir and spruce forests cover its mountainsides. The Bavarian Alps are in the south. They are famous for snowy mountaintops.

Germany has important waterways. These include the North Sea and the Baltic Sea. Major rivers include the Danube and the Rhine.

Did You Know?

In January, the average temperature in Berlin is 35°F (2°C). In July, it is 74°F (23°C).

Königssee is a famous mountain lake in southern Germany. It is known for its green color.

Many types of animals make their homes in Germany. These include quail, geese, hares, chamois, and ibex. Killer whales, dolphins, and porpoises live in the coastal waters.

Germany's land is home to many different plants. Cornflower and edelweiss are two popular flowering plants. Silver birch and Norway spruce trees grow there, too.

SAY IT

chamois
SHA-mee

Germany's mountain areas are home to golden eagles. An eagle is shown on Germany's coat of arms.

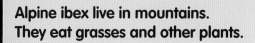

Alpine ibex live in mountains. They eat grasses and other plants.

Earning a Living

Many Germans work in factories. They make cars, food products, paper, cameras, and electronics. Others have service jobs in banking, transportation, or trade. Some help the country's visitors.

Germany has natural **resources**. Coal and salt are mined there. Farmers grow apples, grapes, barley, and potatoes. Pork, eggs, and milk are important products, too.

Germany is known for its car companies. Munich is home to the carmaker BMW.

LIFE IN GERMANY

Germany is a modern country known for its beauty. Some historic cities damaged by **World War II** have been restored. Famous artists, writers, and thinkers have come from this country. German ideas continue to be used by the rest of the world.

Traditional German foods include bread, cheese, pastries, sauerkraut, and sausages such as bratwurst. People drink coffee and milk. Germany is famous for its beer and wine.

Did You Know?

German states were some of the first to set up public schools. In Germany, children must attend school for 9 or 10 years, starting at age 6.

Sauerbraten is a traditional beef roast. It may be served with potato dumplings.

Spaetzle is a German dumpling. It is made from dough, then cooked and served with sauce or butter.

27

Germans enjoy football, or soccer. Cities and towns often have teams, so fans have thousands to choose from! People also enjoy tennis, gymnastics, and track events. Favorite activities are hiking, reading, biking, gardening, swimming, and skiing.

Religion is important in Germany. Many people are Roman Catholic or Lutheran.

People ski in Germany's snowy mountains. They canoe on its lakes and rivers.

FAMOUS FACES

Many talented people are from Germany. Johann Wolfgang von Goethe was a famous writer. He was born on August 28, 1749, in Frankfurt am Main. He is considered one of the most important modern European writers.

Goethe wrote poems, books, and plays. His most famous work is a poem called *Faust*. It is about a man who is saved from the devil. Goethe finished it shortly before he died in 1832.

SAY IT

Johann Wolfgang von Goethe
YOH-hahn VOHLF-gahng fuhn GUR-tuh

30

Goethe was also a scientist.

Germany is known for music. Ludwig van Beethoven wrote some of the world's most famous music. He was born in 1770 in Bonn. No one knows his exact birthday.

Beethoven showed musical talent from a young age. He learned to play the piano, the organ, and the violin. During his life, he wrote many music pieces including nine long pieces called symphonies. Beethoven died in 1827.

Singers, piano players, and other musical groups still perform Beethoven's songs today!

Did You Know?

Over time, Beethoven lost his hearing. He could hear songs only in his head, but he kept writing. He wrote some of his most important music after he could not hear.

Tour Book

Have you ever been to Germany? If you visit the country, here are some places to go and things to do!

 Celebrate

Experience Oktoberfest in Munich. Every fall people gather for parades, rides, music, and traditional foods.

Learn

Visit the Black Forest area, where many German fairy tales are set. Near the town of Wolfach (*right*) is a museum with an old-fashioned farm. It reminds some people of "Hansel and Gretel."

 ## Explore

Take a boat ride on the Rhine River. Look up to see the castles along the river.

 ## Eat

Try sausage, sauerkraut, and other popular German foods!

 ## Play

Go skiing or sledding in the Bavarian Alps! These famous mountains are home to Germany's highest peak, Zugspitze. This peak is about 9,718 feet (2,962 m) high.

A Great Country

The story of Germany is important to our world. The people and places that make up this country offer something special. They help make the world a more beautiful, interesting place.

Triberg Falls is a popular waterfall in southwest Germany. It drops down about 535 feet (163 m).

Germany Up Close

Official Name: Bundesrepublik Deutschland (Federal Republic of Germany)

Flag:

Population (rank): 81,305,856
(July 2012 est.)
(16th most-populated country)

Total Area (rank): 137,847 square miles
(63rd largest country)

Capital: Berlin

Official Language: German

Currency: Euro

Form of Government: Federal republic

National Anthem: Third stanza of "Deutschlandlied" (Song of Germany)

Important Words

capital a city where government leaders meet.
Communist (KAHM-yuh-nihst) of or relating to a form of government in which all or most land and goods are owned by the state. They are then divided among the people based on need.
emperor the male ruler of an empire.
empire a large group of states or countries under one ruler called an emperor or empress.
federal republic a form of government in which the people choose the leader. The central government and the individual states share power.
Holocaust the mass murder of Jews by the Nazis of Germany between 1941 and 1945.
Nazi a member of the National Socialist German Workers Party.
resource a supply of something useful or valued.
unite to come together for purpose or action.
World War I a war fought in Europe from 1914 to 1918.
World War II a war fought in Europe, Asia, and Africa from 1939 to 1945.

Web Sites

To learn more about Germany, visit ABDO Publishing Company online. Web sites about Germany are featured on our Book Links page. These links are routinely monitored and updated to provide the most current information available.

www.abdopublishing.com

Index